I can recognise my letter sounds along with various animals.

This is a simple colourful animal book.

It is ideal for you the parents to use to teach your child about various animals and the letter sounds they begins with .

is for

AFRICA

This is the motherland, many animals live here.

is for

BABOON

They have a shiny red bottom

is for

CHEETAH

They are super fast.

is for

DINGO

They are very vicious.

is for

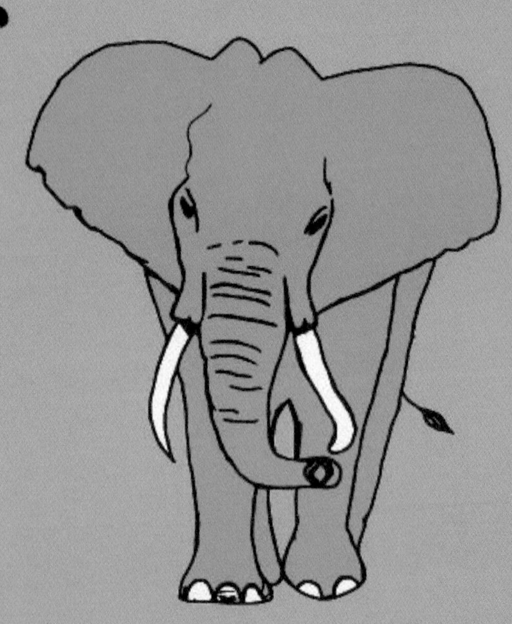

ELEPHANT

They use their trunks to drink water.

is for

FLAMINGO

They usally stand on one leg.

GIRAFFE

They have very long necks.

is for

HIPPO

They are very big.

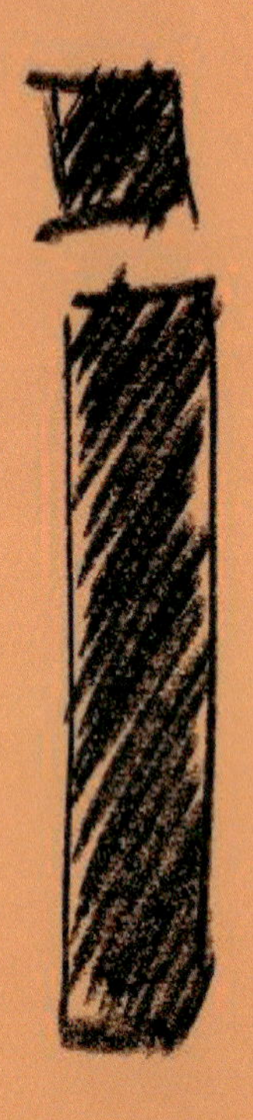

is for

IGUANA

Their colours vary.

is for

JACKAL

They often have fluffy tails..

KANGEROO

They carry their baby in their pouch.

is for

LION

They are the king of the jungle.

is for

MONKEY

They swing from tree to tree.

is for

NEWT

They can regenerate their limbs.

is for

OSTRICH

They have long legs.

They normally hide their head in the sand.

is for

PARROT

They can repeat what is said to them.

is for

QUAIL

They are small birds.

is for

ROOSTER

They canot lay eggs.

This is the hen's job.

is for

SNAKE

They slither around and have no legs.

is for

TIGER

They are the largest wildcat.

Unicorn is a mythical animal all over the world including Africa.

They are ideal animals for
immagination.

is for

VULTURE

They are large birds of prey.

is for

WILDEBEEST

They live in herds.

is for

FOX

They are often very sly.

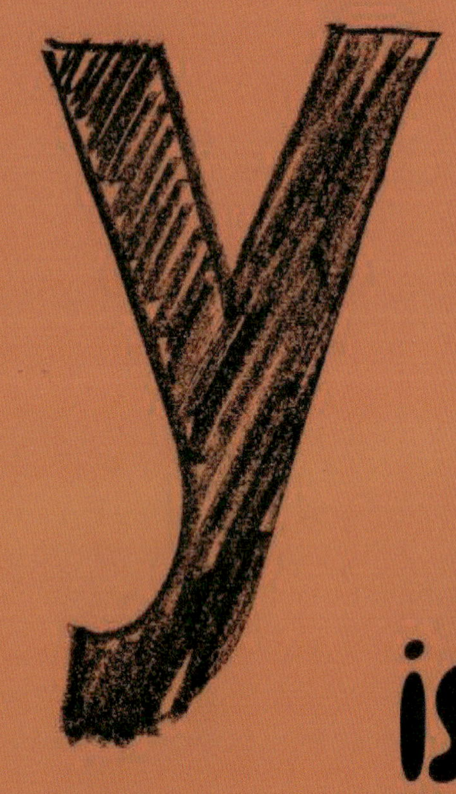

is for

YELLOW MONGOOSE

They are a small african mammal.

is for

ZEBRA

They have black and white stripes.

Different types of animals can be found in different continents all over the world.

Some can be found only in one particular area of the world. While others can be found in various different areas of the world.

You can research and discuss this with your child..

Authored by
Nickela Farquharson

learningreasources@hotmail.com

(More books coming soon)